# ETERNAL
Award Winning Poetry

Edited by Ted Stanley

# HAMMOND HOUSE
### ETERNAL
Award Winning Poetry
Published by
Hammond House Publishing Ltd.
University Centre Grimsby, DN34 5BQ, United Kingdom.

1st Edition: December 2017

ISBN -978-0-9955702-4-5

All rights reserved. No part of this publication may be reproduced, stored in a retrieval system, or transmitted in any form or by any means, electronic, mechanical, photocopying, recording or otherwise, without the permission of the individual authors.

The right of the individual writers to be identified as the author of the work to which they have been attributed in this publication has been asserted in accordance with sections 77 and 78 of the Copyright Designs and Patents act 1988.

Compiled and Edited by Ted Stanley.
Formatting Ravi Ramgati
Marketing: Heather Buckby.
Cover Design: Ted Stanley.

Cover Image from the series *Displacement*, by Deborah Geddes, first exhibited in 2017. Produced by permission of the artist. All rights reserved.

The opinions expressed in this book are entirely those of the individual authors and are not endorsed by the publishers or their sponsors, University Centre Grimsby.

Contains language that may be considered unsuitable for a younger audience.

www.hammondhousepublishing.com

# ETERNAL
## Award Winning Poetry

Enjoy this eclectic collection of poetry that brings together *award-winning* writers from around the world, each with their own unique interpretation of the theme. ETERNAL is the first in a series of poetry anthologies, each featuring a different theme and including the top stories from our annual International Poetry Prize.

Includes the winner of the 2017
International Poetry Prize

'The depth and breadth of this truly imaginative and inspiring body of work reflects the different sectors of society and many regions and countries that have found their way to the University Centre Grimsby to compete in the Hammond house International poetry prize.'

Christopher Sanderson

# TABLE OF CONTENTS

Acknowledgements ................................................................................ vi
Introduction ........................................................................................ vii
Prologue ............................................................................................ viii
No Man's land—Abdurahman Saeed ........................................................ 1
Memories—Alyx Arrowood ..................................................................... 3
Life Eternal—Archie Wilson .................................................................. 10
The Eternal Loop Set to End—Brooke Shamblin ..................................... 12
At the Gates of a New Wonder—Bruce Marshland .................................. 14
The Restaurant of Forever—Caitlin Stobie ............................................. 16
Volbeda—Christopher Sanderson ......................................................... 20
Verse, Colour and Sound—Christina Muresan ....................................... 21
The Village Woman's Song—Daphne Martin ......................................... 22
Infinity Road—David Dixon ................................................................... 27
The Small Strand of the Furthest Reach—Greta Ross ........................... 29
After— Janavi Held ............................................................................... 32
Eternity: The Most Amazing Thing—Janavi Held ................................... 37
A Recipe for Evolutionary Fetish—Jarret Green .................................... 41
Dormition—Konstandinos Mahoney ..................................................... 43
Retreat—Lynn Roulstone ..................................................................... 44
Smile—Mario López—Roldán ................................................................ 46
Hysteria—Melissa Mordi ...................................................................... 62
Stative—Michael A V Edwards .............................................................. 65
The Crossroads—Michelle Politiski ....................................................... 67
Wheesht! – Morag McKinnon ................................................................ 69
The Smallness—Donald Anderson ........................................................ 74
Andĕlka—Paul Ings .............................................................................. 75
Washing Your Corpse—Paul Sutherland ............................................... 76
Eternally Yours—Phillip Burton ............................................................ 78
James Bateman (1811-97) has his Belief in the Eternal
Confirmed by Orchids – Roger Elkin ..................................................... 80
The Choice—Stacey George .................................................................. 82
Immortality—Young Dawkins ............................................................... 83

Sit here,
so I may write
you into a poem
and make you
eternal."

Kamand Kojouri

# ACKNOWLEDGEMENTS

Deborah Geddes, Heather Buckby Ruth Liddlemore, Andy Maughan and the team at Central Services, Hugh Riches and the team at Estuary TV, Leanne Doyle, Jonathon and Katherine Williams-Stanley, Richard Hall, and Michael Edwards. To Simon, Lucy, Carol, and Ella in the University Learning Resource Centre for their continued patience advice and support. The University Centre Grimsby awarding and Kenwick Park Estates for sponsoring the 2017 International Poetry Prize. Competition Judges, Christopher Sanderson, Paul Sutherland, and Robert Petty. Finally, all the writers who submitted such an impressive collection of poetry for this anthology.

# INTRODUCTION

This inaugural year of the International Poetry Prize, sponsored by Kenwick Park Estates and awarded by the University Centre Grimsby, saw an unprecedented number of entries from five continents and over twenty countries which are reflected in the shortlisted poems included in this anthology. Most of entries came from regions across the United Kingdom but submissions were also received from Austria, India, Germany, France, Luxenberg, Denmark, Sweden, Jamaica, Tasmania, Australia, Kuwait, Mallorca, and Estonia. From the USA we had entries from Virginia, California, Connecticut, Colorado and New York. The range of styles and subjects provided a unique insight into diverse cultures and settings around the world and the very high standard of entries challenged the judges, who, unable to agree a final twenty-five, requested that twenty-seven entries be included in the final shortlist.

Thank you to all the writers who explored the theme of Eternal in a myriad of interesting, mysterious and, sometimes, amusing ways. We are privileged to publish such an outstanding collection of work and hope you enjoy this inspiring poetry from around the world.

*Ted Stanley*

# PROLOGUE

It is a wonderful thing to judge a Poetry Competition, you know nothing of the poets, and so you suffer none of the preconceptions that inevitably cloud the reading of poets you already know.

As a Poetry Society member, I suffer (yes I know it's repetition) this every quarter when the Poetry Review booklet lands on my doorstep. So many names I already know, so many words treading the already well-trodden boards, so few new names, so little fresh inspiration.

Of course, in a Competition one accepts that there will be a wide variety of content and quality, especially in this case when the guidelines were very broad.

I hope that everyone who entered, enjoyed the process of constructing their poetry, for it is my belief that the real love which art provides to us, is to take part in the doing, to be the ones writing the words.

It is true though that art needs an audience, and poetry needs an audience. I would love to hear these poems spoken by the writers themselves, their performance I am sure would further lift the words off the page.

But not all Poetry is performance poetry, and in my mind that it is no bad thing; to be able to sit quietly and pour over a set of poems is one of life's treasures, this anthology I am sure will offer that opportunity for many.

We had three judges, each working entirely independently. I then collated the judge's thoughts and tabulated the results. The winning poem was rated very highly by all three judges, but it was a narrow winner, and the margins down the list were ever closer.

As I said at the beginning we didn't know any of the poets, or their backgrounds, but it was obvious, from the depth and the breadth of the poetry, that many different sectors of society had become involved, and many regions and countries had found their way to The University Centre Grimsby, to compete in the Hammond House International Poetry Prize.

*Christopher Sanderson*

# No Man's land

Abdurahman Saeed
United Kingdom

Deep in my thoughts
Absentminded, hands on my forehead
Wondering if there ever will be an end
Trying to figure out right from wrong
At a crossroads, don't know where to go
Time is still, a deadlock situation
A moment of no sense of direction
Wandering in a no man's land
No common place for the common man
A place of wilderness
All at sixes and sevens
Megalomaniac world, detached from reality
Indeed, it is devoid of sanity
I am just a passenger in this spinning world
I am driving into the unknown
With no steering wheel, lacking control
I am just a bystander
Searching for an answer
Arms akimbo wondering what's going on
Not knowing what is in store
Like an unmanned ship in the open sea
Swaying from side to side

Drifting away throughout the day and night
Over the horizon, there is a distant shore
A land of hope, a land to explore
Is it an illusion or a reality?
Is it the promised sanctuary?
The land of roses and rosemary

# Memories

### Alyx Arrowood
### USA

"I Wish I Could Wash The Hickeys Away"
I wish I could wash the hickeys away
It hurts more with every passing day
All the memories and words said
Makes me wish the memories were dead
These words that I'm writing
Can't take the pain away, I'm dying.
My heart hurts from my very core
Every day seems a bore
I have nobody lately
And it's driving me crazy
My body hurts, the marks he left
He stole my heart, a terrible theft
The moments we shared, I'll never forget
The words we said, I'll never forget.
I wish the crying would stop
It just keeps going, nonstop
Why won't it stop? Why won't it stop?!
WHY WON'T IT STOP?!
WHY WON'T IT STOP?!
I want to be happy, forget everything
But I know that won't happen.. I let him use me like a plaything.
Why can't I be happy?
Everything I say and write just has to be so sappy.
The breakup we had, a wrenching heartache
Was it for the best? I want to become opaque.
Not let anybody see the pain inside

Act like I'm fine and walk with pride.
The tears I'm shedding, I want them to stop
The memories I'm thinking, I want them to stop.
The marks he left hurt
A constant reminder of hidden under my t-shirt
I feel like a disgusting
Letting him touch me and always kept discussing
I told him I felt uncomfortable
He wouldn't stop, I told him again, uncomfortable
He stopped.
The times he laid in my lap
I remember them, it hurts my heart like a stab
I can't take this, I don't want to be depressed
It hurts, an unwanted guest.
I keep thinking about him while I wept
Every time I can't help but regret
The way I let him touch me, get under my clothes
Hurts like an open wound that I wish I could close.
The memories, memories, keep coming like an unstoppable force
Crying for hours at a time, my voice is hoarse
I want to scream at the universe, scream and ask them why
Ask them why everything just gets worse
I prayed to god for him, I tried to change.
But he couldn't change, there was no exchange.
When I cut, deeper and worse than usual, all he cared about was how it would mess up our plans.
And how he could touch my thighs with his hands.
I wish I could wash the hickeys away.
Make everything better with every passing day.
I know everything is temporary, but this feels like it'll last an eternity.
I have nobody to talk to.
I'm alone at this time in my life, nobody to run to.
I want to be happy, put on a tougher outer shell.

I don't want to be going through hell.
I still have his shirt, his taste still on my lips.
The way our bodies would intermix.
The readings said everything is going to happen for a reason.
And that the path I'm going down has a reason.
Do I need to let things happen?
Or do I need to control the things before they happen?
The big decision in the end
What will it be? Will it be to end?
I wish I could wash the memories away
I kept pushing people away.
I lost too many people because I he was consuming all my time.
And I lost everybody in a short time.
My stomach is in knots
The medicine I take won't make it stop
I feel sick, like I'm going to die
Maybe I am? It's about time.
I'm not gonna cut.
Not again. I'm not going to cut.
Am I just writing nonsense?
Why am I crying? It makes no sense!
Sure, I miss him. I loved him.
But he let his parents dictate his Actions.
He said he should've ended things 3 months Ago.
Damn. Where did the good times go?
I'm so dehydrated, no tears are coming out anymore.
Why does this always happen? I feel like such a whore.
All the marks..
all the marks..
Yesterday's pain is today's pain.
Today's pain is yesterday's pain.
I'm ashamed of my marks.
These stupid marks.

Every time they hurt
It's a constant reminder of when he had my heart
Hamilton keeps my mind off things
Yet my pillow is still stained as my eyes weep like springs
I can't help but weep
I don't want to weep
I want to forget everything
Forget the pictures, the memories, everything.
You can delete the phone numbers, the pictures, the texts.
But you can't delete the memories, they're buried inside a deep depth.
I told him not to sneak around
But what did he do? Keep doing it and it made us bound.
I need sleep. But I'm still crying
I can't stop crying.
I'll try.. I'll try to forget.
I don't want people to see my pain. It makes me look pathetic. I don't want people to see it. Even if I am
I cry as I write this all alone in my room,
Talking to him again feels nice
It's a bad way to move on the words we say "i love you" are cold like ice.
It feels so wrong yet so right
To want somebody back after only one night.
When we talk, the feeling I get in my stomach is so deep
Sometimes it's so strong.. I can't help but weep.
Something doesn't feel right
Something I can't fight
I want him back, but it's a lost cause
He's moving soon, we can't go back to what was.
What am I doing?
Everything I had loved, the feelings I had.. are slowly but surely undoing.
What am I thinking. I'm completely insane.
I can't think with all this pain.
Every time I remember something we did

It hurts more with each thought it should be forbid.
His family is disgusted by us
They read the texts... everything we had was left in the dust.
When he texted me I felt sick
I didn't know what to say the feeling was so thick.
I let him get in trouble, the blame is on me.
Yet he still refuses to believe.
What am I doing? Am I out of my mind?
Why can't I get him out of my mind?
We want to see each other one last time.
I doubt it'll happen.. but we'll see.. in time.
Why am I still writing? This is all terrible!
I can't express what I'm feeling! It's unbearable!!!
He said he lost his will to live when he lost me
Next time I hear his name it better be followed with a heart beat.
He said he wants to kill himself he's losing his mind.
Can't we go back to when he was mine?
There are two sides to me, take him back, and leave him.
I'm somewhere in the middle.. I'm so confused.. should I be with him?
"Leave him in the dust!" One side says
While the other is still filled with lust.
My mind is drawn a blank. Not sure which side to pick.
When I first got his text I was happy and overwhelmed with wanting to find the old pics.
I did.. and the feeling quickly faded into darkness and confusion.
I haven't slept in days. When will I come to a conclusion?
"I need to hug him one last time" one side begs.
"No! You're weak! Be strong and forget him!" The other says.
Why are you still stuck on him? I don't understand..
the feelings you had.. left when he tried to make you understand..
He left.. the feelings left.. yet some still remain.
Deep in my stomach with every thought of them just brings more pain.
I cry as I write this all alone in my room,

The softer side taking over.
My eyes and feelings just seem to spillover.
What are these feelings? Sadness? Shame? Hurt? Mad? Confused?
Confused..
Maybe it's a mix of all 5 all coming at me at once.
Yet the feeling still remains deep down within.. I remember when they were free once..
Last week.. the times before that.. all were better than this.
I miss going to school with him and seeing him everyday. What the hell is wrong with me?! My feelings seem to have dropped into an abyss.
He cursed me when he stole my heart.. but I wouldn't wish for anything else than to have him back in my arms.
There we go again, the grieving part of me comes out.
But oh no, here comes the confused side. The ones that hurts the most... crawling it's way out.
I cry while I write this all alone in my room,
I want to text him and tell him to come back..
but he's asleep by now.. and I don't want to seem like just some annoying brat.
I don't want to admit to myself that I miss him, I don't want to cry.
The more I hold it back.. the more I die.
Am I being over dramatic?
Or is this just another fanatic?
My writings are something I may never show..
For they hold the pain inside. Something I cannot show..
I can't admit how much I want him,
He broke my heart, yet somehow the feelings remain.
Something wrong.. what's Happening inside my brain?
What are these feelings I feel?
I've never felt this before.. is this a big deal?
I keep remembering the day he left.. waking up late (6pm) and getting his text.
It broke my heart. I soon began to weep.

Why am I wearing his shirt? Why do I still care?
What is wrong with me.. why am I so scared?
These feelings are all new.. something unexpected.
When will they go away.. their presence is not respected.
This is all so confusing.. what does it mean?
Why can't I just wash myself clean?
The thoughts of us being sexual, something we loved.
Soon became something we couldn't bear to think about.. something far away, shoved.
I feel like a slut. Maybe I am.
I feel like a slut.
Well, I'm running out of words and running out of time.
Even though the dreadful pit in my stomach still remains.
I guess we will have to stay in our own lanes..
He's one of the best thing that's ever happened to me. He taught me how to love myself. But as soon as he left.. I began to doubt myself..
Is this all my fault? I'm sure it is.

# Life Eternal

### Archie Wilson
### United Kingdom

Her fingers were speckled like
brown chicken's eggs.
They felt both hard and soft,
sticks in tissue paper.
Her veins were ruptured; rivers
on a decaying landscape.

The room was hot and dark
and smelled of ancient secrets.
Granny's smell; I wrinkled my nose.
She tried to smile through
her agony, to make me less
afraid as I fidgeted in the chair.

Be a good boy for your mother;
Her gossamer voice, barely audible
reached across time and touched me.
She needs you son, look after her.
I nodded, bewildered by this mystery
but full of dreadful wonder.

Are you dying nanny? Sotto Voce.
Mummy says for me to kiss you.
Come then son, kiss me on the cheek.
I was hesitant and afraid. She lifted my
child's hand and gently touched it
with bloodless yet tender lips.

Are you dying nanny? I don't want you
you to die. The tears welled unbidden.
No my child, how can I die when
I live on through you, my beautiful
grandson. My life is rich and eternal.
I did not understand and was
uncertain.

Next day brought an empty bed and
a world of empty hearts.
Now, a lifetime on, it is I in the room
waiting for the circle to turn. I drift
in morphine haze and pray
my granddaughter will understand.

I hear the tiny tap on the door and
try to smile so she is not afraid.
She enters, thumb in mouth
and I want to cry for her. I try
to speak but can only croak. I
reach out and see that my fingers
are like brown speckled eggs.

# The Eternal Loop Set to End

Brooke Shamblin
USA

three born, two married, one dead

Life and Death met again at the crossroads and held hands.
You know Life said *I'll never know why I've lasted so long*
**It's because the gifts you create strive to stay and hide from me**
    *Yes, for some reason they are afraid of you.*

Their meetings marked by each star,
for them, these times were a rare blessing.
There were times when they would have just long enough
to dance in the time between no life and no death.

You know Life said *I'll never know why I've lasted so long*
Death brought Life into a tight embrace
    **Yes, for some reason they are afraid of you**
Death took in a deep breath, **afraid of you leaving with me**
    one born, three married, two dead

Since the beginning, they were always each other's' gift.
Never a kiss shared, but satisfied as
their eternal love story set to begin at the end.
They wait till the day the sky runs out of room.

Death brought Life into a tight embrace,
Life broke away with the same sadness in her eyes.

Death took in a deep breath, **afraid of you leaving with me**
**You see** Death whispered, **when you die, I will walk with you**

Never a kiss shared, but satisfied as
there were times when they would have just long enough.
They wait till the day the sky runs out of room,
their meetings marked by each star.
        two born, one married, three dead

Life broke away with the same sadness in her eyes
*It is because the gifts you create strive to stay and hide from me*
**You see** Death whispered **when you die, I will walk with you**
Life and Death met again at the crossroads and held hands.

## At the Gates of a New Wonder
Agra, Uttar Pradesh, India

Bruce Marshland
USA

Death brings such beauty
    and beauty such death.

Inches beyond spitting distance
    from the gardens of memory,
clusters of men in variously soiled linens
stand, squat, and stoop, watching tourists
    enter a realm of white marble.

Those who came to wonder become objects
to be wondered at.

At road-side, extended families seek
shade among tarpaulins and cardboard,
    which they call home. The old
        blink a seemingly eternal siesta,
the young scrambling for coins in the dirt
begging favours from passing strangers,
    oblivious that beyond the gates,
a fortune that would feed a small nation
    has been lavished on stone chambers
        for a member of the gone.

Social asymmetry provides an antonym
    to the balanced domes of Shah Jahan.

Our rupees gain us entry to the tomb
        and a marginally vandalised kingdom.

All things come to dust,
           even the dead,

but this new wonder of the world rejoices

that in mortality is cause for celebration.


So soon the Taj will collapse into ancientry
        like the ruins at Halicarnassus, and we
           may find ourselves asking Mumtaz why

she ranked first among her husband's wives.


For now, though, we must gawp at an archway
        to another empire, squinting after shadows

that forged ahead like tour leaders, untouchable
        to us, like the men outside on the road.

## The Restaurant of Forever

Caitlin Stobie
United Kingdom

Third Place in the 2017 International Poetry Prize
University Centre Grimsby


Madame, monsieur, good evening

and welcome to Forever.

I am the maitre d'.

May I show you to your seat?


I can't give you the best table;

Father Time's been sitting there

for the last few millennia,

drowning himself in whiskey.


I heard Mother Nature stood him up.

And before you get comfortable, I must ask you to pay

no attention to Shakespeare.

He's been slumped in that corner


longer than anyone remembers,

saying something about summer

to the fake flowers

between glasses of gin.


But here in Forever,

we welcome the ones who wear black

to traffic light parties.
We reserve tables for those

who search years for someone
who won't make them wait.
Our cutlery is melted-down promise rings,
donated by pregnant schoolgirls.

The chairs are upholstered
with wished-upon eyelashes.
Our napkins are Dear John letters
that were never delivered.

And the menu! The house wine
has a palate of promises, best served chilled.
Our dish of the day is regret; it comes
with a side of bitterness.

You can taste the last time you stood
in your childhood house
and felt at home.
But our after-dinner mints are as sweet

as the birth pangs of a wife
who only knows miscarriages.
Our bills are written with
invisible wedding invitation ink.

We peel paint off the walls

of every high school art room
and graffiti our doors with
the words you wish you'd said.

We make masterpieces
of the memory
of the last time
your father looked you in the eyes.

And at the back table,
between lost handbags and coats that used to fit,
we record all the great romances
that should have been.

So let today be the day you enter.
May it be the day you remember
the names you rehearsed
when you fell asleep.

Today, forget that pain
is more than a sheet of glass.
Let it be the day you put memories
into lungs
into breaths
into voices
into songs
so you may throw them all to the wind.

This is where you'll find them.

Stay as long as you need —
the restaurant is always open.
Come inside.

# Volbeda

### Christopher Sanderson
### United Kingdom

He paints from memory
He walks across the machair
Out to the still or raging seas
On to the living sands
Back in his studio he lets
The canvas carry his load
He works from memory
The depths of his distant
Unconscious are ravaged
Whilst his present mood
Reflects in the surface
Tension of the painting

These will be original
Works from memory
For as Jac says 'He is
A professional artist
He is a painter
Not a printmaker'

# Verse, Colour and Sound

Christina Muresan
United Kingdom

Second Place in the 2017 International Poetry Prize
University Centre Grimsby

I think about inspiration and its source
and how it takes me by surprise
like the time I was listening to a live guitar piece
by a composer I knew nothing about
too powerful and unusual to analyze
So I close my eyes and
listen in deep silence
and a thought comes to me like a gentle wave
it says this music sounds like a Dali's painting
It makes me smile in its weirdness
only to find out later that Dali and the composer had been friends
I try to understand where that thought came from
so I think about Jung's archetypes and the unconscious
and about Einstein who was simply playing
in the garden when he discovered the theory of relativity
I know there is a link
between my verse, Dali's colours and
the musician's notes
maybe they are golden dust
from a cosmic mandala
that my brain is too small to grasp
so I settle for gratitude.

# The Village Woman's Song.
(Malawi. Early twentieth century.)

Daphne Martin
Malloca

**Part One: Preparing fields and finding food.**

The sun was rousing cockerels as I walked the mile or so
to the place where, come the rainstorms, my chimanga I shall grow.
I'm excavating furrows and it's hard, exhausting work,
but unless we want to starve next year, it's toil I mustn't shirk.
My baby boy was sleeping on my bouncing, straining back.
He seems to like the jolts and jerks – the badza's sudden 'THWACK!'

A search for firewood followed next. Three daughters helped with that.
Their brothers came along as well, with traps for hare and rat.
Young Jong, the greedy, sharp-eyed brat, yelled gladly: "Look! I've found
a great cement-like pinnacle – a whopping termite mound."
We framed the hill with bendy boughs, all woven-in with leaves,
to stake our claim upon the ants and warn potential thieves.
And later, when the downpours come, and insects start to hatch,
a well-placed pot will yield, we hope, a luscious , scrumptious catch.

Then Esther saw some zumba leaves ... Ecstatic sighs arose;
and quickly, since they're good to eat, we stripped the bush of those.
I'll dry them in the sunshine, and then bind them into balls
to use when other produce fails, or on our palate palls.
Our people think they're toothsome, so they sample as they pass.
I have to guard the drying leaves, or hide them in long grass.

**Part Two: Fetching water from the dry river bed in the valley below.**

When noonday's heat has sizzled past, our drinking jug is void.
How water seems to *melt* away! I sometimes get annoyed.
The dambo's dry and dusty. The river's simply sand.
Small droplets slowly seeping serve to damp the hole we've panned.
With gourds on handles long and straight we scoop with practised skill.
(Our daily gossip's never rushed. The pots take 'hours' to fill.)
The bailer dips, and gleams, and drips, until it's time to raise
a jar upon each woman's head and wend our homeward ways.

Up powd'ry paths plod bare, cracked feet. In slow and stately line
we pad past Proteas parched and pale to reach the hill's long spine.
Bright dresses blink twixt mottled trunks, and pause on frequent bends.
Talk dies. With gaps expanding wide, the moving line ex - tends.
'Explosions' flare above our heads: – Msasa's russet tints
delight the eye for miles around with rain-portending glints.

Banana clumps appear at last; then chicken coops on stilts,
Our granaries (all empty now) have lids at curious tilts. in marvellous *autumnal* tints!)
We're glad to see the village huts. Their thick-thatched roofs provide
an umber shade that's almost chill – beside the glare outside.
My shuttered home is cool and dim, secure from scorching shafts,
while open doors, one front, one back, catch brisk refreshing draughts.
Each day I dump my burden, and I rest beneath low eaves.
The ledge of mud that's round the house my weary frame receives.

## Part Three: Afternoon

Today relaxing thus with friends, our fingers husking nuts,
I watched the boys play 'bottle tops' between the village huts,
and heard my mother curse their noise - redoubtable old crone...
Her wrinkled face does call to mind an avocado stone.
The interlude was brief, alas! – The sun keeps moving round.
Since then I've swept, patched Lennard's shirt , some brewing millet ground.

I've pounded the cassava roots (a fibrous, heavy job
although my daughters skinned it first) and now it's on the hob.
As soon as bubbles rise and pop I'll snatch it off the heat.
It burns at once, and then it's just *impossible* to eat.
At best it's slimy, smelly. Ugh! It's *not* our fav'rite food!
No wonder when cassava's served all spirits are subdued.
Our maize ran out a month ago; so what we do is try
to camouflage makaka's taste with relish. And we *sigh*!

N-diwo's salty savour, if well-prepared and panned
adheres to rolled n-sima balls but not the dipping hand.
Potato, bean, and pumpkin leaves make sauces we esteem.
(We grow them in the valley when there's water in the stream.)
But now, with rains still yet-to-come, green gardens there are none.
No cultivated plants are seen. Our dried ones, too, are done.

## Part Four: More about food.

And so we go and forage for our foodstuffs in the wild;
for fungi, termites, tubers, leaves – chipwete , if they're mild.

We sometimes find M-phala lines a-creeping up a tree,
or fat grey crickets, buried deep, small boys unearth with glee.
The red-winged, lurching locusts (large), green flying hoppers too,
we boil or fry. We find they make a very tasty stew.
If someone goes to town or lake he may bring back some fish.
Fresh, smoked or dried – when simmered up it forms a zestful dish.

Limanda leaves we bubble fast in water drained through ash.
It turns the dende bitter but, with added peanut mash,
tomatoes (two) and crystal salt... it won't be *quite* so rough.
The potash water, there's no doubt, does make the leaves less tough.

### Part Five: Day's end

My caref'lly stirred n-sima I will smooth into a dome
and place it with the spicy dish on mats beside our home.
I'll serve the meal at sundown. The men will get the best,
and if they think the food is good their group will talk and jest.
But when it's hard or bitter – they're *not* a happy crew.
However, when supplies are short, there's nothing we can do.
The things we've somehow grown or picked we give the male elite
while women, children, dogs and pigs get what the men won't eat.
It's seldom any scraps remain, but when they do, we're gay
for on the morrow they will serve for nibbles through the day.

When sunset's flaming glory burns the boundless, satin sky
and echoing up the valley shrills the jackal's haunting cry...
When fires, no longer tended, cease their twinkling from the hills,
and glow worms try to take their place, while heav'n with starlight fills

our talk will wane and falter, and the slatted wooden bed
will call us – for the day is done. Another lies ahead.

# Infinity Road

## David Dixon
## United Kingdom

It was a warm summer night took my thoughts to the park
Where the blossom and cicadas blew my senses apart.
My head was kinda spinning then came a tune
It was Bob Dylan singing about the 'Man in the Moon.'
Tried to keep focused but my mind was weak
Then I picked up the tempo got in time with the beat.
The bats in the belfry sang 'you gotta keep cool!'
Spun around did a moonwalk said 'I ain't no fool!'

The yellow moon was dancing on the ripples of the lake
Delivered like a pizza from the fickle hand of fate.
Got a painting in the attic it's a 'Dorian Gray,'
Gotta stop this ageing process there must be a way.
Got to thinking of the moggy that lives down our street,
Twenty years old, believes she's still an athlete.
That's the way to do it, gotta think like a cat
Gotta get the attitude of this urban acrobat.

I was mooching down an alley in a bootsellers souk,
Got suckered by a booter who flogged me a book.
It was full of strange symbols runes and rhymes
And the 'Fountain of Youth' was printed on the spine.
Decoded the meanings, deciphered the signs,

Followed the clues, read between the lines.
It was signed by the author who'd scribbled 'I lied!'
'Drink 'Auld Nessie Whisky' if ye seek eternal life!'

Well I eat right, sleep right, workout in the gym.
Changed my way of thinking; turned veg'e'ta'rian.
Enrolled on an meditrial, 'youth serum' course,
Got an instant lift and tuck and a head of golden curls.
They spun out the double helix in my genetic code,
Then spliced in a hybrid geno called 'Infinity Road.'
Now I'm surfing down this highway so 'Never say Die'
Till you meet the 'Head Honcho' up there in the sky.

# The Small Strand of the Furthest Reach

Greta Ross
United Kingdom

Winner of the 2017 International Poetry Prize
University Centre Grimsby


At the horizon's wink the sky links silver with the sea,
threads a drifted ship to a hair's breadth from a star
and winds a whispered foam of fear round each sailor's soul.
Now *the vast and possible ocean* settles to steal
Ulysses from his longed for homeland and sets
him wayward bound for Ulixbona's rock-fast shore.

*Black roofs of the end of the world* rise at the shore
of this uncharted land where storm gods stalk the sea,
angels trail ash from sun-charred wings, and the moon sets
loose night's demons to light the still Pole star.
With the Devil's breath Ulysses' ship cuts through the steel
cold skin of the sea as it takes the measure of his soul.

*Myth is the nought that means all,* for all is soul
wrote Pessoa toeing the edge of dissipation's shore
while paper heroes sailed with Titans to steal
the mists from Uí Breasail or tame with spells Antillia's sea
where bishops found a phantom isle by a fictioned star:
seven bejewelled cities remapped by warring mindsets.

*You rise in the sun within me and the mist ends* when Selene sets,
he whispers to the ocean lulled in folds of velvet, and lets one sole
sigh undulate along his sleeping ship and slide across a star.
At daybreak the ocean hears the tumult of drownings at her shore,
unravels the hissing foam from Ulysses' foundered ship to see
*the gods of the storm and the giants of the earth* steal

his sailors' breath, salt brittling their bones, rusting their steel.
At first light Pessoa scours the seabed for syllables and signs, sets
down: *'the dream consists in seeing the invisible shapes'* and the sea
responds with the heartbeat of her waves, the give and take of her soul.
He charts his horoscope, foretells his future by the fall of light on the
shore and writes of Magellan, da Gama, and sea-faring kings who follow
their star.

Ulysses wills the day's horizon to stitch his galleon to the North star
to outwit Poseidon's rage, then to reel him through Hell with a line of
steel.
He places a stone cross on *the small strand of the furthest reach*, the shore
of Pessoa's Ulixbona, a *padrão* to stake a claim for centuries of sunsets.
*'All is worthwhile when the spirit is not small'* wheel the constellations as his
soul flies the perimeter of the impossible to encompass the vast Atlantic
sea.

At life's end Pessoa pursues his Gemini sign and sets his personae free
to mimic Ulysses' ploy: to be Nobody yet in poetry live in every soul.
At Lisbon's shore he enters salt and air to forever sail his Portuguese
Sea.

Notes
1. The italicised phrases are fragments from Fernando Pessoa's cycle of poems, 'Portuguese Sea'
2. *padrão* = a stone cross inscribed with Portugal's coat of arms placed on land claimed by Portuguese explorers.

# After

Janavi Held
USA

After faint hopes
and long vigils.
After eternal loss
and protected ashes.
After wood
and dead ships
in the night.
After testimony
to affirm worship.
After oblivion
and quantity.
After enduring days
and impossible nights.
After times funeral
and fugitive shadows,
science and weapons
and weeping.
After glorious twilights
and perfume.
After wavering children.
After the edge of resistance.
After loud destruction.

After the silver of ceremony.
After bedrooms
and the uniforms of trees,
tranquility, and thirsty lips,
and complicated substance
and human beings
and nowadays
and clothes
and arms and legs.
After smoke and sand.
After lamentations
and degraded doubts.
After death
what?

After constant victory
and perpetual failure.
After the increase and decrease
of populations
and the circulation of darkness.
After propaganda
and human armies.
After accumulating
and rotating and solitude.
After witness and execution
and night returning.
After fusion

a portrait
a sunken face
a cold wind.
After expansions
and extensions.
After the depths
of desertion.
After faithful widows
and mud
and overturned intentions.
After death
what?

After the rotation of the multitudes
and bodies and chaos.
After cruelty and punishment.
After pomegranate mornings
and harvest nights
and the buildings like mountains.
After today what?

After residence
and passage
and deciphered nothings.
After geography and empty isolation.
After ancestors and religions.
After violent mourning.
After the dust.

After the unspoken sings.
After the fire.
After awakening love
what?

After the drunken bones of intoxication.
After repetition, repetition, after repetition
what?

After desecrating the dead
and celebrations
and enlightenment
and clear water
and the slaves of time.
After farewells
and tears
and engraved guns
and the bloody altars of time.
After invasions
and humbled nations.
After slaves and murders
and the eyelids of blindness.
After mirrors
and mortality.
After pity.
After martyrdom
and serpents,
and the demolished ashes of the rose.

After the immortality of stars
and the fire of avarice, the corpse,
the spared day, the sterile seconds,
dampness and tools.
After the city,
and the fearful weight of naked time.
After vanity and wine.
After laughter
and dying
What?

After the immunity of innocence.
After the determination of greed.
After lust.
After the dance is done.
After healing.
After shaking loose.
After karma.
After eternity
what?

# Eternity: The Most Amazing Thing

Janavi Held
USA

The question of existence
is an overwhelming
city of shadows and patterns
it is difficult to speak here
inside this great flickering
wall of smoke.
Speaking what I'm meant to say
I will always remain unpopular
to those educated in seconds
rather than in eternity
but I have always existed
soliciting the ethereal prudence
until now not responding
to the rumors of the spiritual rebels
or the controlling hands
of inconvenient death
that invisible benefactor of hours.
Downwards and upwards
all empty as a desert cistern
the exhausting decay of it all
like weeds covering a cracked grave
or rooftops burdened
with too much weather
overgrown, shambles
life in exile

what is unspoken
and unheard
folded into a sheath
of redemptions
as tears tumble
grinding out knowledge
and ignorance.

What is worthy of rain?
Those dry rocks? My heart
sitting in a un-stilled silence?
Or the Divine Name in exile
from the lips of would be
lovers and friends?
How can I endure that
which they do not hear?
Our kingdom is crumbling
under the clutch of evidence
not different from death.
I am not mocking the saints
and the things they always say
about how tomorrow and
today contain eternity
I am saying that life
is not like a decaying river
waiting for feel-good psychology
to educate the public
spring just is
with its cool wind and
opening flowers
as it gives way to the

god of summer heat
it just is, like the shape of my bones
and the Timekeeper of my breath.

Inside too many churches
God has been abandoned.
Instead there lives the
determination of the seasons
circling between good and evil
nothing is as ready to rotate
perpetually with vacant morals
like empty eyes
eternity remains unspoken
and I am sad without you
who have no taste for sky
but only for what exists in-between
beginnings and endings
and all movements which walk
towards perpetual demise.


Without proper poetry
there really is no peace
just as it is impossible to
build a home on rotten timbers
tall, silhouetted against
an effortless, invisible sky
how can we continue to live
without a visible sanctuary?
I can't resurrect the universe
as it is and all its

overwhelming questions
but I can speak with thunder here
in the privacy of my thoughts.
I can remember that I exist
as proven by the
apparatus of consciousness
and the coolness of my heart
as it descends into that easy infinity
and all the information
and evidence that lives there
which I arrive at when
ignorance and passion are silenced
by the thirst for knowledge and affection
because here on this terra-firma
love is a flickering, twisting flame
which will go out
without the eternal breath
of the Soul of all things.

# A Recipe for Evolutionary Fetish

Jarret green
USA

(Sensory deprivation)

Blindfolded, she feels heat
animate static gray planes.
Spilled chaotic sugar feeds
organisms without central nervous
systems. The surface cools.
At 400° Kelvin, bacteria evolve
into multi-celled organisms.

(Evolutionary amelioration)

Gagged, she pulls stainless steel
atoms with her teeth,
cutting through minerals.
Her gleaming tabula rasa
stretches over distance and time:
flesh ready for purple supernovas.

(Vacuum preparation)

Bound, she breaths deep carbon
dioxide, cosmic dust. Organic
hawser flattens her universe: sticky

shiny, starry latex monolith slices
her perceived infinity, cruelly
collides into veins and ligaments.

(Ambulatory limitation)

Eternity cracks against her
outstretched hands. Venus's
round mantle erupts: violent
mosaic of pink blood.

Ascended, submissive, she becomes
intelligent life ready for instruction:

*Roll dough into a tight ball.*
*Make a flat circle with your fists.*
*Assimilate gas molecules into a density*
*outweighing their gravity:*
*Drop to your knees and crawl*
*into the remnant core.*

# Dormition

### Konstandinos Mahoney
### United Kingdom

Weak from fasting she walks across hot stones
to a sea so crystalline you can see shoals of fish
patrolling its shallows. Holding her hands,

he coaxes her in right up to her breasts,
tilts her gently sideways off her feet.
Eyes closed against the high summer sun

on the soft springs of his fingers she rests supine.
Slowly he let's go, leaving her suspended
like a conjuror's assistant -

a lifelong fear of water, at an end.

The daughter holds her breath, slips under,
sees the keel of her mother's back,
her open arms, the cross of her shadow.

The fragrant scent of pine drifts on a breeze,
the pulsing chant of the cicada swells in adoration.
Face framed by a blinding halo,

soon she will wake up and step ashore.

• *In Greek Orthodoxy, The Dormition of the Theotokos on August 15$^{th}$, celebrates the 'falling asleep' of the Virgin Mary before being taken up to heaven and eternal life.*

# Retreat

Lynn Roulstone
United Kingdom

The coiled edges disappear
under the greenery.
Spikes of loosestrife and lupin
rise from the tangled grass.
Overhead, electricity
hisses across the wires.

Between the two,
we walk.
Each in our silence,
we smile and slip past.
Moving to the
empty paths
when we meet.

It is the campion
that draws me back.
Always the campion
Red splashes
on silver.


Under the trees,

conifer and cedar,
It is damp.
On the other side
lorries clatter.
Here it is still,
apart from startled birds,
breaking,
from the trees

It is the campion
That draws me back.
Faded, pressed
into my notebook.
Red splashes
on silver.

# Smile

Mario López-Roldán
France


Smile.
The pulse of the world
is still beating. Time
has forgiven itself. Urgency
died peacefully.

And now
everything is smiling at you.
The wind of million blessings
is chasing you again. Stop thinking,
stop moving,
smile.

I am amazed again
with your perfume life.
I say you love me bluntly. I say
you kiss me on the mouth every summer,
every diamond winter, but again
every spring and every fall.

Smile, there are so many beautiful deeds
looking for you like hunting dogs,
delightful surprises surfing to you
like the unstoppable sea waves, fizzy love
alive and windy like an embrace from the unifier
living you today here

while you smile.

Smile,
the garden is full of roses,
the monster has dropped your case,
a hundred sharks protect
your arms and legs.
You dominate the essence that goes
beyond your thoughts.

Smile again.
You are an ice cream, a fountain
of the divine, a fish swimming
and dancing
for the simple felicity of being.

You are forgetting
your fears, the clouds
are but friendly tensions, you smile and
you water down your state of against.
God is you
when you smile.
You flower torpedo,
you connected chancer,
you megalo burst of confidence
hanging from the mastil of redemption.
Show me your teeth, crunch your eyes,
smell the flowers of now.

Across the eleventh day inside your
idea of exception, you enlightened

all faces with a smile.
You are the universe ambassador
you are the stars that are the
fish in the dark high ocean
living and dying.

You are
the crazy wind, free
and smiling, you posses
and receive everything,
you are the song of Poseidona and Atlas,
you bloody warrior of love,
good luck is born in you every
time you open your eyes and every
time you close them.
So smile you world class smiler,
for so many presents
are waiting for you to open them,
so many legs
and breasts still about to celebrate your
hands of eagle feathers.

The only faulty cloud
is your mind, the only shooting frontier
is there, and the all time freedom also
and it all makes sense
in that smile; that precious juicy fruit
tempting all.

Pain is blurred by laughter.
So soon all your prejudices will

melt like ice in Crete. Smile then,
the skeleton is the temple
of your aliveness. You pray
to the night singing, pray to joy like
a marathon of light and grace.

Growing in you, life
assumes a lovely faulty perfection
in a smile. Flowing in you,
throughout a crazy smile,
life is the bridge
between the formless and the form.

Smile, driven by inclusive silhouettes
beyond your sword fish body
bridging the best
sunset through
the best sunrise. Smile, you pirate of God,
you crowned mountain,
you splendor made swimmer.

Underwater, smile. Over sunshine, smile.
In deep darkness, smile.
In airports and stadiums,
in hospitals and discotheques, also inside,
inside, inside, in golden light
smile!


The atom of delight
is gripping your foot.

It is a soft night, bloom of heaven,
blooming dances, ripping
the day off, a drug,
a new language a veredict of feel good feeling.

A story to be told
from seduction to intuition,
a copy of your senses
turned into your inside out.

If not smiling, then shouting around,
I am full of life juice,
lights and dreams that will make
you become what you wished
the day you were turned down
by fortune.

Don't be afraid.
Be the dance,
the opal, the moonstone of
music and emotional lava
you flying fisherman of smiles.

Smile you clever animal,
hang crazy collars
from your neck. Surprise in
its lightest form will cry your name,
and if you know how to wait
you will spend the divine coins
in the right silk,
in the right smile, in the right

insignificant heaven.

No surface would be strong
enough for your soft pressure,
no sense of room will ever compound
your frustration into sand, your moisture into love.

I can,
I can, I can, is the song of the
living patriarch.
The smile, it is your smile,
the ultimate compassion.

So smile and elevate
your jumps to the lines
traced by seagulls on a tall blue sky,
elevate your joy to the level of falling stars, jump
when you can, live jumping and smiling.

Stop doubting with a smile,
you can, you are everything,
stop looking around, the target is
in your silent smile,
in your perfect design as a walking lung.

Good luck is your voice,
and after touching other hearts
it will ricochet like a boomerang
from Apollo alive.

A smile breeds a smile,
a start is a start. A smile

is a volcanic force conceived to improve
what exists.
It is the metaphor,
the molecule, the emphasis of
renewal. A smile is enough.

A stone is always necessary
to change the route of the stars,
a stone is a solid smile, a stone is
a frozen smile so alive,
a stone is the act of smiling

So carry a stone in your pocket
to connect with deeper conscience, for no
approval is requested
from that magic in you
and only by mixing your
ease and your groove.

I will insist then, smile. Kiss
that formless mouth,
bite heavens, love the stranger and
the route as magic
tokens or positive bullets
that kill your ego.

Shot your ego, embrace the formless
say "is that so?"
No science, no sream
will take you beyond the power
of presence smiling.

Open the heart of real music,
blow up your lungs with oxygen
like Zen balloons and love.

Smile then beloved friend,
feel the hot stones
that your naked feet are blessing,
run upwards, reach out
and touch a thousand souls,
release the hunger of love,
distill life in every minute,
like nitrogen in music.

Like transparent liberty in
sensual waters,
for a smile is the blessed nucleus
of good luck,
the primary sperm of communication and
understanding. Become
a human translator, smile again.

Smile, undo the undone,
rip the curve in a frozen beer,
swing all sounds
in ascending waves of joy unfolding,
feel your body, feel
your friend beside you, smile.

Kiss your fate, indoors,
outdoors, walking
and swimming, and stopping

and thinking, smile and trigger
the quantic energy that holds
everything together.

Be the benefit of your gift,
be the surrounding magic of your
good luck, become
a castle of light, smiling
for there is no reason to lose
any hope.

Dream our movement,
dream your future,
create yourself humbly, silently,
discretely smile.
Restart the engines of life and love,
take off again,
heaven is waiting for your iced stars.

Smile this morning
you "good for me" human,
love your steps like water,
love your heaps like high tech,
drum up yourself,
bass down yourself to laughter.
Accept what is now.


To the enemy, smile,
to the foreigner, smile,
to the passing dog and the believer.

Squeeze your chlorophyll out
of your self-confidence
and give it away always for free.

Jump into your secret being
and trap it. Become
that fantasy and be
that pure light, to the wind, to the moon,
to the absurdity of finance and
the naive arrogance of economists,
smile and switch on the booster of acceptance,
the amplifier of forgiveness,
the equalizer of love.

Take yourself on a crazy ride through
an invisible ocean of aliveness.
Enjoy change, suck up change,
understand change,
smile to it like a wise guru of stillness,
smile to it like a mountain smiles,
like a nuclear missile
of certainty and trust.

Smile at change,
embrace its beautiful message of
allrightness. You are
a conversation between your dreams
and your fears, live it
as a wonderful experiment of
evolution, like a loop
of spiritual ascension in a smile.

Like a cocktail, like a
warm fire at winter,
smile like fig trees do,
pouring out sweet generosity,
smiling to yourself like expanding
emptines until it becomes you,
all you, smile.

Archer of time, fear nothing, lift
your trust high, throw yourself
into the wildness
of taking what comes as what should be,
smile to the traps, to the disease,
to competition, smile to them
as you smile to you.

Throw your scare to the dogs
and laugh. Send your doubt to
the lions and smell how it smells.
No doubt you are more than
what you want to reach,
no doubt you can walk your talk.

There is a crazy strong energy
ruling everything
underneath all and surely it is flowing
to your advantage, so smile to that energy.
Smile to your children, smile to all children,
play with them as a ritual,
as a sacred mythological legend.

Your smile can change everything.
Listen to the sound of your soul, listen to
the sound of your veins, listen
how you cut the wind like a happy sail
when you smile. Drop the weight,
drop the unnecessary burden.

Open yourself like a window,
wide open,
wider, wider, when
you smile to adversity randomly,
a wide open window, when
you smile to fatality rebooting,
wide open widow, when
you smell the smoke and
jump off the deck smiling, when
you smile by mistake,
by conviction, by faith and reflex,
smile, and paint the world new.

When you smile you matter. The rest
doesn't matter. Dance and smile,
that's the greatest freedom,
soaking compassion
blooming, that's the biggest magnet,
the greatest
illusion, you are a kyte.

So smile when you can,
like a cold glass of ouzo
whitening the ice of life, like a roaming

cloud full of water, like a kyte of
certainty.

Try to forget your past, and really try, try,
you are more than any memory or grievance,
you are not what you think you fear,
you are the link to the eternal,
the stars inside the ocean,
so smile. Dream wide. Breathe like the space,
put yourself in your own shoes.

Declassify all information, all secret codes,
all cells and walls will fall to your feet
when you smile like thunder,
like a firefly in the dark,
like a dolphin jumping and losing control.
Smile, dam it.

Celebrate this now,
life is being prepared for you
like a party, life is
your birthday party. Dance! Splash!
Celebrate as you know, as you can,
as you may, as it is made for you
like a higher purpose.

And when it is over
you will be full and be prepared
to start again. So smile like a tree also
to the idea of death
even when it scares you. Smile

and redemption will
sweep fear away like morning fog.

Smile you squid of love, your body
is full of oceans, your trumpets
are announcing the permanent spring.
No hesitation in a smile, no loss
of trust, no ego.

When the mind is taking over,
smile and go back
to the real you, to the formless flow,
pure happiness, wind whistling, spices
flavouring, rock not afraid smiling.
The smile is your passport to you.
Don't let the mind fool you
you green cliff overlooking the waves singing,
don't let the mind
deceive you one more time,
you are a port and a hundred boats are
entering you with the best flowers and spices
from around the earth. You shine!

That smile will connect you
to the best part of everyone
and everything, it is a speed boat
to our common roots and dreams,
our dotted lines,
our tuned and un-tuned chords.

Smile and kiss

heaven in drums and dreamland, for
all the world shines like a pack of fish
in shallow seas when that rescue fluid
drops from your golden eyes.
The speed of sound
is growing as I write.

Smile with all your body and presence
you swinging seagull
and crack the thunder in two.
Remember deep
into your changes and smile.
You wind of seaweeds,
you water of forbidden deserts, try
the unimagined, your smile is a compass.

Go find the summer again, smile and
lose the pain in your feet,
smile and rain on
thirsty crops at dawn, smile
and forget your bearings
for you are a rose, a mermaid, and a bat
dislocating death as a bad thing.


Smile you delirious part of me
who doesn't believe in any greatest luck
than smiling and the absence of fear
will conquer your life forever,
and your body and mind will be just a part
of you, and the positive flow of life

will flow in you, and you will be the needed
light aligned with the wholeness of
universal being smiling at
your natural state
of permanent connectedness.

Now!

# Hysteria

Melissa Mordi
United Kingdom

A weird year
Filled with tire skidding and school girl binge drinking
travel bottles of spirits under desks
Candy hearts crushed under soccer boots
And orange gingham bras glowing through transparent white button up shirts
Backyard poolside glass Cola bottles
Pink lipgloss and red lipstick
Pushed down socks over battered Mary Janes
And school skirts rolled up to pierced belly buttons
Newly grown breasts flapping against too small chest
While streaking under stars in the park
Spin the bottle squat and piss over pregnancy tests
Hair tangling between sleeping bags whispering secrets
Flashing old men who stare too long
And holding our breath under car dashboards with mouths full of
Boys boys boys
In musk sweat and soapbox glory
Drugstore romeos who we crush and sniff like pharmaceuticals
To ignore the too old men who stare too long
We chew, suck, and spit tobacco girls in jars we hide in too tight jean pockets

And write our names in steam over mirrors

And scratch our hopes in bathroom stall walls

We kissed ourselves under movie star spotlights

And touched ourselves in dark theatre halls

We burnt our tongues with rainbow sticker lighters

And blew pink gum like the bubble could never burst.

We carried ourselves like balloons

And pushed manicured nails down throats

Till we weighed less than air

And stored insecurity in the spaces between our ribs

And licked boys lips for calories

We fed on fresh meat

And marked our predator status with highlights

We chewed, sucked and spat out tobacco girls

Who eyes hid behind rose coloured smoke screens

And clung to childhood hair clips

We balanced at the top of the world in stilettos

And wiped spider leg mascara tracks with latex condoms and report card letters

We birthed galaxies in our ovaries and bled them out

Onto stranger's sheets and shut our eyes and stretched our arms in speeding cars

And peeled pieces of ourselves off school desks

And ran naked through the streets screaming

And kissed necks under bleachers

And bleached our hair under gas station taps

And stuffed gas station chocolate inside too big bags

And watched rain tap on glass
Over and over again
We burned the world with kisses
And slept in other people's skin
And stretched ourselves too thin
Over playground pavements and schoolyard crushes
And as light as balloons we floated
Away to lonelier blue skies till
one day
we woke up.

# Stative

### Michael A V Edwards
### United kingdom

It's time

How quickly the night has passed

My company of ghosts

Tormented that which I could not conceal

Knowledge of my guilt did not shield me

Still they will come

I listen for the sound

That which I dread to hear

Caustic blood navigate my veins

Will it hurt?

Does it really matter?

What was that?

Calm, calm yourself

It's just….what?

Why do I waste my time!

I have so little, yet I waste it

I think of all those lazy days

Sleeping in till noon

Waking with thunder in my brain

What I would give for those moments now

I would not waste them this time

If I stare at the hands of the clock…

Don't try to fool yourself
You can't hold back time
*JANGLE OF KEYS!*
*MY GOD!*

# The Crossroads

### Michelle Politiski
### USA

At the ripe age of 18, there is a crossroads -
An inevitable halt where screeches are unleashed
From the wheels...and our hands crush the steering wheel
And we are hyperaware, for a moment, of the buildings
And the smoke that clogs the horizon.
We are overwhelmed with a ravaging type of guilt.

We don't know quite what to do with this guilt,
So tell me: what is the key to the crossroads
So that we may unlock a horizon
Where maybe, finally, our efforts can be unleashed
And we don't shamefully enter buildings
Dragging behind us an accident of a steering wheel?

Tell me where we can repair this steering wheel,
Tell me where we can resolve and dissolve this guilt
We feel...for what, exactly? Climbing buildings?
I refuse to believe the crossroads
Is a place for demons to be unleashed
Because I tell you, I see too much green on the horizon.

Tell me! Recount me a time you watched the horizon
After just a slight turn of the steering wheel

And you watched before your eyes as your soul unleashed…
And just for a second, there was no guilt.
There need not be this dusty, ugly crossroads
Where we must decide among nonexistent buildings.

I believe every day I walk through buildings
That speckle the coast of my state, its horizon
Flecked with absurdities that the demons decided at the crossroads
When some poor soul jerked to the right his steering wheel.
But sure, they need not feel any guilt
As though our youth's worst nightmares were not just unleashed.

I know in my heart of hearts you wish to unleash
The growls that howl behind the doors of your building.
You can't ignore them, but neither can you ignore the guilt
You are owed to feel for what kind of pristine horizon
You tarnished when you dragged me your broken steering wheel
And promised me!--you had seen no crossroads.

I won't make you feel guilt, because the foreseeable horizon
Will do it for me, and will unleash and spit out from your building
That broken steering wheel that you swore! Has never seen the crossroads.
I wish you were lying.

# Wheesht!

Morag McKinnon
United Kingdom


The Kirk spawned their meeting that cold Sabbath morn,
by encouraging presbyters to greet a false dawn.
Fifi came home with Ma, then elected to stay
for the preaching of Jesus, for wooin' Ma, Faye.
Ma changed when Fi came, but I canna remember
just how good, or how long was the peace that November.
We watched as their eyes met, took heed of the prayers
that they spake oot in tongues, ignoring the glares
of the Factor, the Manse… and, Ma falters here…
Och, we no ken the reason folks holler, Yous queer!
And the hissing grew louder, alerting all Bute
to gather as one and condemn Fifi's suit.

By Rothesay & Bannatyne the innocents went knocking,
blessing zelates & glibglags and all who were mocking.
The jeering of lads as they gang down the road,
and scandalised parents, who were thirsting to goad
Faye and Fifi apart. Deemed their loving a sin,
forgot they dishonoured the Pier Master's kin.
A'feart was our Granda, Bute's Pier Master and wife
of black demons of vanity, of hell fire, of life,
of love and forgiving, of senses salacious,

of all the Wee Free would condemn as rapacious.

For 'til then Ma's short life had been sensibly dour
her diversion, the kirk, when Pa James was on tour.
Soon James quarrelled with Fifi and the Pier Master came
in fine navy serge he called out Pa James......
'bout his drinking, his women, his heathenish singing,
his vows before God, his derisible cringing.
Our Granda was roaring "You've ruined oor Faye".
Curst roundly our Pa, the crooner James Crae.
The Pastor came running, then the Pier Master's quack,
and we frittering bairns were fast hurried back
from the tears of our Ma who, now standing alone,
tore the beads at her neck, and strangled a moan.
Our Grandmammy fainted; the doctor was craven
"Dinnae fash yersel Faye for it'll be a haven,
Lochgilphead's nae distance and soon you'll be hame."
How could we know then that the day never came.

Heaven hangs dreich as we girded ourselves
against hell icing over when the Procurator delves
into Ma's madness, and Grandmammy's drinking,
at Edinburgh High Court, as daylight was sinking.
The Pier Master stood straight for to redeem his wife,
"She's feckled her ways, sworn the Pledge on her life,
Oor duty's tae Faye, tak'd awa under section
Fur madness, nae badness, nae need for correction."

Back then Mother was ten, Mags nine, Jimmy just two
when they brought them together and bade them on cue,
to say who they'd choose to care for them now
that the tree has been felled, who'll cherish the bough?
And they looked to their Father, where else should they turn
for succour and solace when wanting to gurn.
So James took them away from the Pier Master's wife,
but put them with carers he paid for in Fife.

James lived for himself, for his fans, for his money:
For a sensuous life, one spread thick with honey.
Aye, they wandered the globe, just he and his mistress,
His three bairns were left, depressive and listless.
Free in the New World James squandered his fortune
then sailed home to Greenock, all set to importune
his wife's Ma and Pa. Only then did he learn,
how they'd perished together, out by the burn
as they prayed for their sins and those of their daughter
locked up, far from home, racked with mental disorder.
They died with their love and their fear all a dither.
Grandbairns, a daughter, left trammelled to wither
and die for forever, in a strange understanding
of mothers, and fathers, and gods all commanding.

My own Mother stares at me now. Her harsh hazel eyes
and her slash of a mouth were no stranger to lies.
She'd told of my sister who'd died from the hunger
that passed on to me and into my number.

But instead of consoling and laying to rest
the death of her firstborn, by doing her best
to shield me, support me, as only she might -
from the plight of my infant - she simply took flight.
Still, I'd listened, believed her, I'd lived with her pain
and all through her lying feared I was insane.
'Til Dad told me the secret of Faye's incarceration,
the role of my Mother in Grandmammy's privation
from the world, from my life, until that April day
Her brother sent new of their mad mother, Faye.

There was trouble the day that the postie man came -
Revenge. Serve it cold. Assign it her name.
Mother came home. I told her. She started to cry.
Now sixteen, I abused her for daring to try
to grieve for a mother she'd only once seen,
since the day she'd been my age - some twenty years e'en.
She'd denied us our ken of the kin that had fetched us,
exposed all her kirk's Weeness,
its classified Freeness
as a pit that was stinking,
as a bane on men thinking.

I stood tall before her, encircled her throat
and told her to shut it, like she were a stoat.
For here she was gurning, sustaining her grief
at perfidious mothering, whose time had been brief.
Oh, shamefully all I could do was to hate

one already so bitter that no one could bait
or befriend… No, nor trust her again.
But the truth of it all is I am still her wain.

And now as I look to my ain folk and me,
and reflect on their lives, how came it to be
that the sorrows corrupting our distaff generations
crush'd our will to resist their perverse perturbations.
How the madness embraced us. Yes, more than a few.
And the dancing, the drinking, the whoreing of two
more narcissitically nurtured, 'til one tied a noose –
absorbed in an image he could not shake loose.
He yearned for his mother. Mags was Faye's second child.
She was feckless and starstruck and ran rather wild.

Kirst's nature was nurtured in our Mother's guilt.
I miss her, my sister, and the tears that were spilt.
Kirst was not their firstborn, nor second nor last.
Her misfortune? The role into which she was cast.
To set myself free from this maternal mendacity
At eight I embraced TB's timeless tenacity.
And when Mother died Kirst ascended her throne.
Told the polis Dad died through my caring alone.
This cut was much deeper, much bloodier by far
than any before. Perchance, on a par
with a grief I'd imagined Kirst always forswore,
but as lime on a wound, it burns livid and raw….

## The Smallness

Donald Anderson
Scotland

Growing old I shall not weep
at being small, then smaller, vanishing
into something less than a particle
in this old universe
that may be infinite
or else an atom in a greater 'all'
like a tenement with rooms
above, below, across or through the wall,
filled with families we do not encounter,
unseen neighbours.

I've put on Bruckner's seventh:
millions upon millions of vibrations
to make a cathedral of sound.
Bruckner – on his knees before his God,
holding to a faith I cannot share
except in what I hear
granted him by heaven – so he would say –
something he knew
of smallness, vastness and eternity
that might be true.

# Andělka

Paul Ings
Czechia


Ease through visually unfathomable spreads of lipstick
with lips; unsmear a way in
for the sticky was merely the outer film.

Powder-soft or downy-hair-soft the skin so soft now
it's not till the cheek bone's adamance we know
we've come up against it all, passed right through

all multiple degrees of separation
caked in and fume-zoned under a hair of pop art
more stiff hat on top than effusive outpouring of heaven.

No period of thought's finger-tip-to-chin-dimple was required.
No ankle held atop knee in a stylized backward lean into a reclining chair;
this is not flirtation [friend: the human universe on open].

You've dipped your finger in a pool of years:
poky-poke at its surface tension - it popped effortlessly -
forward lean into the zone of the glow of poignant delight

held in two hands like a rare goblet, a relic, and bulk
starts up its laugh in spills and splashes swashbuckling eyeflash.
Forever means backwards as well as forwards my friend.

## Washing Your Corpse

Paul Sutherland
United Kingdom


I wash across your black and blue forehead
wrinkled; rinse out into a shallow bowl
and pat and stroke with a damp face cloth
your purple nose, inside your ear's whorls
and back around your stubbled chin, over
collapsed cheeks to your brow's under-edge
then ease my flannel round off-colour eyes,
a yellowish moss oozing from these ovals -
is this what tears over a lifetime become?

I'm careful, maybe too careful. I don't want
to damage anything: who knows how easy
it is to puncture a collar bone's slack skin?
I wipe your arms, into the concavities of your
elbows, then the top and bottom of your wrist,
no pulse of course, back up your pitted right arm.
My white gloved hand slides round each finger
across ten old nails like blackened beaches.

I am taking too long, but I can't rush this
labour. I want to un-soil your every location.
Each fibrous dip and rise, each creased opening
and viscid closure – (who knows why?) as if

details have meaning, I'm giving you dignity
down to your feet, bending to a last practicality -
attaching name and age - I fasten with string
a brown label not too tightly to your big toe.

# Eternally Yours

Phillip Burton
United Kingdom

Poetry was in your blood, sinews, shoes
and you sought the widest audience.
For preference you'd speak to the ocean
all day if permitted. I bundled you away
for the sake of the kiosk lady and a seagull.
That's enough, Darling, for today.

You made notes with a shrunken hand
as though there were no space
for your calligraphy to dilate further.
You wrote a teenage novel, back of a card
(*A Lady in Waiting*, Johannes Vermeer).

From Newcastle station and a staid café
I bundled you off to college. You wrote home
when I sent you a pen. At half term
we shared the battlements of Berwick, arm-in-arm
the way prisoner and guard can appear to do.

I bundled you onto a platform
where you improvised verse for the cinder track
and would have climbed under the Virgin train
to witness the sleepers awake.

Autumn. A thin show of beach-life —
a bundle of stone for seafront repair.

By midwinter, your writing hand
had spawned a wild italic, launched off
your own pad, and with loops like the orbit of Mars.

Constantly being bundled (up off on)
    had proved quick to undo.
You'd fleshed-out a new hero, Andre Wee
whose graphite lines ramble but flower at last
    in a sitter's perfect likeness.

## James Bateman (1811-97) has his Belief in the Eternal Confirmed by Orchids
Roger Elkin
United Kingdom

Devoted to collecting from aged eight,
Bateman spent a fortune, not to mention
others' lives, satisfying his desires.
So, invested days page-grazing
plant catalogues, or rolling the globe
locating places - Guatemala, Surinam –
to trace the plants inhabiting his passion,
till he became entranced by petals
as skin-thin as newborn flesh with its mesh
of skyblue veins barely formed.

How he desired those sublimely white,
their buds like rows of graded baby toes,
their clown-sad eyes lighting brightly
under full sunshine or ghosting through
slow twilights where he lingered, fingering
stems, and smelling their must.
And how he lusted
after the shockingly exotic in jamborees
of colour from the Creator's palette, almost
frantic in their patterning, so obviously foreign
in enviable beyondness they warmed

his table-talk with the wonders of the Lord.

He could sense their tendrils spreading,
as he strolled past, and their roots - spotty,
blotched – lifting, spidering out, seeking
leverage in the mossy compost, the cradling
bark, and, believing their leaves to be the panting
tongues from the angels of his imagining,
was convinced he could hear their breathing,
so knew, just knew, their petal-wings angled
after him, mouths agape in silent adoration.
His. Theirs. God's making. God's sport.

"Ferns and other flowerless plants came early in the Divine programme, because the coal, into which they were ultimately to be converted had need to be long accumulating for the future comfort and civilization of our race, while the genesis of Orchids was postponed until the time drew near when, Man, who was to be soothed by the gentle influence of their beauty, was about to appear on the scene."

James Bateman, Introduction to Monograph of Odontoglossum, (1864-74)

# The Choice

Stacey George
United Kingdom

You choose me to be your mother
In a place without any time.
Knowing we will teach each other,
We wait for the stars to align.

In a place without any time,
I choose you to be my daughter.
We wait for the stars to align
With your first breath out of water.

I choose you to be my daughter,
But in this life I'm not aware.
With your first breath out of water,
There's an eternity we share.

But in this life I'm not aware
A choice was made outside of here.
There's an eternity we share
With nothing to lose, or to fear.
A choice was made outside of here,
Knowing we will teach each other.
With nothing to lose, or to fear,
You choose me to be your mother.

# Immortality

### Young Dawkins
### Tasmania

Imagine knowing
something there
even when it isn't

like the air you can't see
but breath and
love
a color not possible

yet painted forever
in the pictures
you make
when you finally
close your tired eyes
and sleep
like your own
sweet child.

And what if real
was even more real
truer than
you ever knew

and every morning

it came to you
always.

Then would you believe?

# HAMMOND HOUSE

A social enterprise membership organisation founded by students at the University Centre Grimsby and run by volunteers. We aim to encourage and support creative talent in art and literature providing opportunities for members to showcase their work and develop a successful career.

Our current activities include Publishing, Literary Competitions, Film Making, TV Production, Writing Workshop, Festivals and Community Engagement Programmes.

Members benefit from reduced competitions fees, and opportunities to showcase their work or get involved in our range of creative activities.

We are planning to offer a range of publishing options to new writers, and expand our programme of engaging with isolated people in both rural and urban the communities through art and literature.

www.hammondhousepublishing.co

## University Centre Grimsby

## 2017
## International Poetry Prize

The inaugural year of this prestigious literary prize saw a record number of entries from five continents.

**WINNER**
The Small Strand of the Furthest Reach by Greta Ross

2nd Place    Verse Colour and Sound        Christina Muresan
3rd Place    The Restaurant of Forever     Caitlin Stobie

The twenty-seven short listed entries are published in this anthology for you to enjoy.

JUDGES - Christopher Sanderson, Robert Petty and Paul Sutherland

Sponsored by

KENWICK PARK ESTATE
Golf Hotel and Spa

**HAMMOND HOUSE**

# 2018
## International Poetry Prize
### 1st Prize £ 100
### 2nd £50  3rd £25

Worldwide Publication
for the top twenty-five entries

---

Entries open 1st January 2018
Submission deadline 30th August 2018

---

OTHER 2018 COMPETITIONS

International Short Story Prize
Annual Screenwriting Competition

www.hammondhousepublishing.com

The University Centre Grimsby, as part of the Grimsby Institute, is built on high expectations, a focus on learning, commitment to achievement and an engaged, practical education for all students. A wide range of degree level courses are available including BA (Hons) Creative and Professional Writing.

www.grimsby.ac.uk

## KENWICK PARK ESTATE
### Golf Hotel and Spa

Country house hotel in 320 acres of woodlands, parks, and manicured grounds with woodland lodges, club spa, evergreen spa, tennis courts and championship golf course. The perfect place to relax and recuperate

www.kenwickpark.co.uk

# BILLBOARD TV
Theatre, Music, Movies, Art and Literature

BILLBOARD is produced by members of the Hammond House group at the University Centre Grimsby, including students from the creative arts, media and writing faculties, graduates, and members of the local community.

The programme covers Theatre, Music, Arts and Literature across the Humber region, going behind the scenes of your favourite shows, reviewing the latest film releases, books and art exhibitions, interviewing local celebrities and showcasing local musicians.

Billboard provides a great opportunity to showcase member's skills and pursue the Hammond House mission to encourage local talent and engage with the local people.

Broadcast on regional television and always available at www.billboardtv.uk

Estuary TV - Channel 7 - Freeview 8 - Virgin Media 159

www.billboardtv.uk

# HAMMOND HOUSE

## OTHER PUBLICATIONS

ETERNAL – Award-Winning short stories - 50 cleverly conceived and entertaining stories from around the world.

CONFICT - Award-Winning short stories from our 2017 International Literary Prize.

WHO'S AFRAID OF THE DARK - Illustrated children's story featuring augmented reality.

SHAKESPEARE IN DEBT - Hilarious Elizabethan farce.

## FORTHCOMING FILMS

SPIN – An uncover police woman is torn between love and duty. Featuring a replica of one of the most expensive cars in the world, the Ferrari 250 GT Short Wheel Base California.

EIGHT BALL – Winner of the 2018 University Centre Grimsby, International Screenplay Prize. Candidate for the Asthetica Film Festival.

www.hammondhousepublishing.com

www.ingramcontent.com/pod-product-compliance
Lightning Source LLC
Chambersburg PA
CBHW030455010526
44118CB00011B/941